The dismissal of an employee - HR knowledge for Managers

Knowing is not enough – One must also apply.
Wanting is not enough - one must also do.

Johann Wolfgang von Goethe

Christian Müller

The dismissal of an employee - HR knowledge for Managers

© 2017 Christian Mueller

This oeuvre takes into account the legal status of January 2017. The author has prepared the contents with utmost care. However, liability for any inaccuracies is excluded and the oeuvre does not serve to replace counseling in individual cases.

Impressum
Christian Müller
Saint-Priest-Str. 1
63165 Mühlheim am Main
GERMANY
cm-hrmanagement@outlook.com

Content

Introduction 8
Termination as a last resort 10
The Criticism discussion 11
The warning 14
The dismissal 18
    Ordinary dismissal 19
        Person-related dismissal 22
        Conduct - related dismissal 25
    Extraordinary dismissal 26
    Dismissal on suspicious ground 27
    Altered condition of employment–related dismissal 28
    Probationary period dismissal 29
    Special protection against dismissal 30
    Exemption 33
    Notice of dismissal 35
    Employee's possible legal actions 36
        The Labor Court 37
    The Cancellation Agreement as an alternative to dismissal 40
The exit interview 42
    Phase 1: Termination and justification 46
    Phase 2: Dealing with emotions 48
    Phase 3: Focus on the future 51
    52
The internal communication 53
The withdrawal 55
The dismissal - an image killer wrongly performed 60
The reference letter 62
Why is dismissal valid? 65
Cost of terminating an employment contract 68
Conclusion 71
Important legal extracts 72
    Protection Against Dismissal Act (PADA) 72
    § 1 Socially unjustified dismissals 72
    § 1a Claim for Severance Payment for Operational Grounds – related Dismissal 73
    § 2 Modified Conditions of Employment – related Dismissal 74

§ 4 **Seeking Redress in the Labor Court** 74
Work constitution Act 75
    § 95 Selection Guidelines 75
    § 102 Co-determination in the case of dismissal 76
    § 103 Exceptional dismissal and transfer in special cases 77
Civil Code 79
    § 622 Notice periods in the case of employment relationships 79
    § 623 Written form of termination 80
    § 626 Termination without notice for a compelling reason 80
    § 630 Duty to provide a reference 80
The Author 81

Introduction

"Whoever wishes to lead can also be dismissed." A very provocative sentence, which is been refused or seems surprising to many managers. Besides the desirable effects on popular areas such as attitudes and salary increases, the role of the disciplinary supervisor also includes strict performance and workforce management. A dismissal is a demanding and important management task; It is the hardest disciplinary tool made available to a manager. However in practice, managers try to exclude this part of their tasks regularly or entrust its implementation to other staffs. This is often the case where employee's announcements are made by the human resources department, without the manager at least attending the meeting. This does not make sense in the context of personnel management, for dismissal is considered a non-delegable managerial task. Upon a dismissal process, the manager is often confronted with facial and emotional discomfort. On one hand, this can be due to the fact that he does not totally agree with the decision or on the other hand, that the dismissal has considerable economic disadvantages for the employee. Upon discussions with managers, it is also known that the communication with the rest of the team is often perceived as difficult. Questions such as "Will my decision be supported?", "Am I now the evil one?" Or "Is my team still pulling?" are used by many managers. Another reason is often uncertainty due to lack of knowledge in the dismissal procedure. Many managers also shy away from talking to the employee in which they open the notice. The issue of dismissal is usually negatively attested and is often delayed, although a termination is unavoidable in purely factual terms.

    As a manager, this book gives you the knowledge required to prepare a dismissal, to distinguish the various types of dismissals, how to conduct an exit interview and issues to consider regarding the termination of an employment relationship. This book will enable you discuss at eye level with your human resources department, a lawyer or similar partners who legally accompanies the termination process. You have to be equipped with the necessary expertise to confidently engage a conversation with your employee.

Termination as a last resort

Why is the term "termination" actually pronounced? Termination is always pronounced when the employment contract cannot be maintained. This can be based on the fact that the employee can no longer be employed, thus jobs are been cut or restructured and employees with other qualification profiles are needed, or still, when the employee is considered no longer tenable by the company if in any way he wrongly behaved or for personal reasons making further employment impossible.

In Germany, the employment contract is under the protection of various laws which protects the employee from the arbitrariness of the employer. Thus, dismissal is always the last resort, the so-called "ultima ratio", whereby, following a conflict between employer and employee, the employer should first use all other means at his disposal to settle the conflict.

In the following, we will access the termination process from the very beginning for a better understanding about: the warning, the various types of termination, special cases in the termination process, the notice of dismissal and the Labor Court process until to the employee's departure and the issuing of the reference letter from the employer.

The Criticism discussion

There will always be conflicts where people work together. This definitely seems important to a certain extent because conflicts can lead to new aspects of cooperation. However, a certain standard of interpersonal conflicts is defined for the smooth running of the work processes and as a guarantee of work quality and order. Certain rules should be prescribed among other things as an integral part of the employment contract whereby if there are deviations, you must intervene as a manager as early as possible. In certain cases, small conflicts or unwanted behaviors addressed at the earliest possible time can be quickly and easily eliminated. The later you will react as a manager, the less understanding the employee will have. The legitimate question he then poses is: "Why my behavior wasn't objectionable in the last few weeks, but addressed today?"

In practice, common mistake is been used in many companies as the sole feedback platform during annual discussions. Reason being that, throughout the year, managers do not engage solely in issues of employee dismissal and performance management but then, once a year as they must seize the opportunity and report back everything they noticed throughout the year. However, Performance management is only useful as a continuous process and should therefore be carried out on an ongoing basis. For the annual discussion, the performance is often kept within the scope of a variable compensation system with an impact on remuneration. So the critical discussion is not only an important instrument within the performance management, It is also the first step when it comes to preparing a termination or avoiding it.

It wouldn't be both appropriately human and economical being directly disciplinary upon a minor misconduct and to issue a warning for example. On the other hand, you should rather provide time as a manager and talk with the employee. As mentioned earlier, this should take place in a timely manner; a quick reaction has to show to all consistency and with which employees cannot carry out what they wants. Surely most people always go as far as one leaves them with no supervision.

How should such a discussion be held? It is important that the conversation does not take place spontaneously and informally. Take your time; talk with your co-worker, in a quiet and behind closed doors. In order to make the conversation as emotion-free as possible and without a direct accusation, we recommend the guidelines below. When preparing the conversation, you should focus on the formulation of this problem by identifying notably or bringing out concretely the misconduct. In addition, you should be aware of the improvement you expect. However, nothing seems worse than describing your observation to the employee, sharing this observation, asking what he can do better, and you receive no answer. Here you should be able to clearly communicate your vision which is also hard for many. A feedback like "It cannot go" or "This is so wrong" is prepared quickly, but does not designate the desired behavior or the desired ideal condition.

Guide:
1. An opening entry like: It's good that you are here and we are talking to each other.
2. I've noticed that ..
3. That makes me / us ..., ensure that ...
4. Because ...
5. My wish for the future is that ..
6. The advantage this has for you / for the others / for us would be that ...

These sentences form the basis of your feedback discussion. They refer to the most important: the description of the misconduct, the effect it has on you as a person and the organization, the explanation of why this works, and the appeal for improvement in the future as well as their positive effects.

Invigoratingly, a conversation might look as following:

"I noticed that some of the invoices you created in the countercheck still got mistakes. This makes me a bit sorrowful, since the bills are a business card of the company. When errors are committed, this can be a bad light on our company. Furthermore, we must make a correction of the invoice and get our money later. I would hope for the future that you work here more carefully, check everything again before it goes out, so that the invoice will be more error-free in the future. If the invoicing runs smoothly, I can trust in your performance and later on assign you further exciting tasks. "

Furthermore, you can provide your support:

"Is there any points that are unclear when you are invoiced? How can we support you? "

Note that criticism should be well used. If you are in a permanent criticism mode, this will frustrate the employee and he will become more passive. Excessively criticized employees do not trust themselves any more to decision making and become dependent. Working by rule and the attempt to delegate the manager's tasks can be the result. Use criticism for important things and do not grumble due to banter situations. After a while, you should in return notify the employee if you notice an improvement. So he sees that on one hand you are not only experiencing negative things, but also, that the concern is so important to you.

The warning

Based on the criticism discussion; presented in the previous chapter, if no improvement is observed in the behavior, do not pronounce a termination yet. Once again, termination should be the last resort, the ultima ratio. The Labor Courts attach great importance to adherence to the Ultima Ratio rule. As a rule, they require a warning in the case of a behavioral termination. A behavioral or an ordinary dismissal without any warning before a court is virtually without a chance.

So what is a warning? A warning is first of all a warning to the employee that he has to reckon with consequences; if his behavior does not change. With mere threats of disciplinary actions, the employee is therefore informed that a continued violation of the tasks specified in the warning can result in a termination of the employment relationship. More also, upon indicating the misconduct of the employee directly renews his chances to improve on his behavior. Furthermore, the warning provides a documentation function which is a breach of the employee's contractual obligations. It is basically not form-bound and can also be given orally. However, in practice it is mostly given in writing and archived in the personal file. The written form ensures that a definite proof is available in later disputes and the content can be clearly stated.

The warning should be given promptly; as soon as the employer learns of a new misconduct. The employer should pronounce the warning and if he leaves a lot of time between the event and the warning, the warning will lose its effect. Firstly, the employee certainly will not change his behavior significantly if several months have elapsed between the incident and the warning. In certain circumstances, he cannot even recall the facts in detail. More to that, the legal effect of the warning gets lost if the record of warning is not clear and properly applied, than it could have been if duly and promptly warned. A good rule of thumb is a two-week period between the identification of the violation and the warning.

> If a warning has been held for some time between one to three years depending on the severity of the breach, if the employee is seen to behave henceforth in a faultless manner, this warning can no longer be used for dismissal.

Points which an effective warning must include?

Component	Reasoning
Herewith we would like to remind you	The warning must be recognizable as a warning. Also use the subject line to include the word "warning".
On April 23, 2015 at 9:00 am, you were met in workshop 2 in the final assembly area without personal protective equipment.	The misconduct must be clearly identified with time and place. It must be comprehensible for third parties.
This contravenes the occupational health and safety regulations, in particular against the instruction XI / BC dated 21.06.2012, which an integral part of your employment contract.	The warning must make it clear that there is a violation of a valid internal directive, company agreement, and prescription or the employment contract.
We hereby request you to comply with the abovementioned instruction.	The warning must demand an immediate adjustment of the misconduct.
In the event of a repeated breach, you must expect further employment consequences up to termination.	The consequences of continuing the misconduct must be demonstrated so that a termination in the next step is legal.

If the behavior of the employee does not change after the warning has been issued, you can still consider issuing a warning which the tonality should be marked clearly and to concretely threaten the termination. This is particularly advisable if the deliberate event is not very critical, but still disturbs the operating sequence. However, if the warning record is very critical and has been documented accordingly, the employee should be dismissed in the next step.

In summary, the warning is a milder disciplinary instrument of the employer in contrast to dismissal and which is usually to be used before the ordinary dismissal is terminated.

The dismissal

Firstly, let's consider what kinds of dismisals are there. We distinguish between ordinary and extraordinary dismissals.

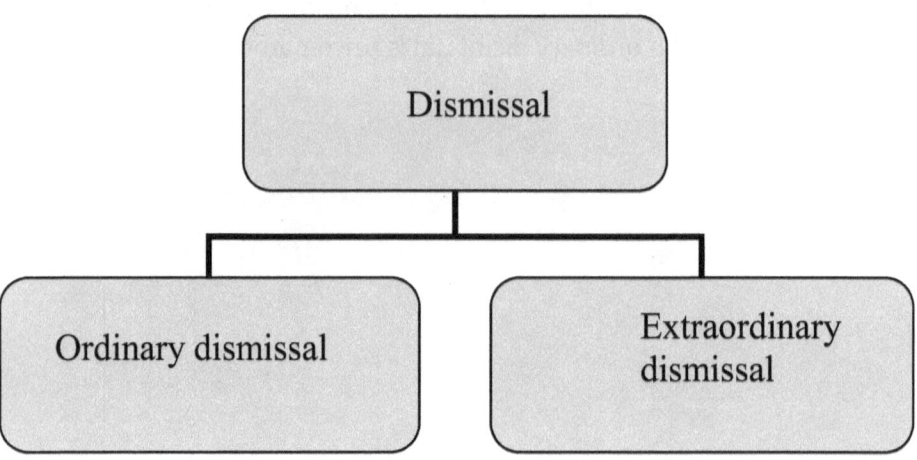

The termination is fundamentally a unilateral declaration of intent and requires a written form (§623 BGB).

Ordinary dismissal

The ordinary dismissal always implies that the employment contract is been terminated considering the contractual and statutory periods, and the protective laws. The notice periods is initially derived from §622 PADA, but can differ by a valid collective agreement (possibly disadvantageous or not) or work by contract (only for the employee betterment). The deadline for dismissal within the probationary period is generally different. In addition, other periods of notice may also apply to certain groups of persons, for example for the severely handicapped according to §86 SGB IX or apprentices according to §22 BBiG.

In the case of ordinary dismissal, the law also distinguishes between three types, depending on the reason for the termination.

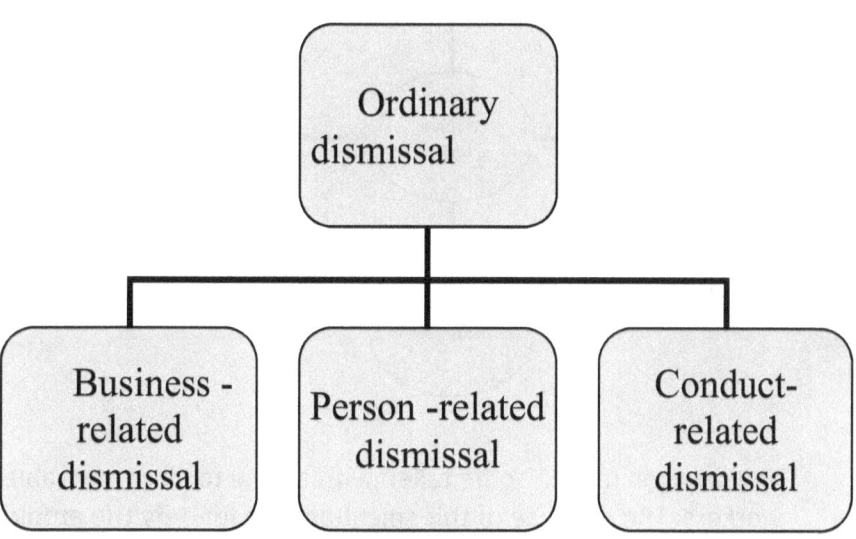

Business - related dismissal

The reason for the Business - related dismissal lies within business or operational requirements. Business-related termination assumes that the position of the employee can no longer be made available to the workplace. However, the employer is obliged to make the selection of workers to be dismissed on social justified aspects and also to check whether further employment is possible at another position in the company. For the socially justified selection (social selection), the following criteria must be considered:

- Age
- Period of employment
- maintenance obligation
- Disabilities

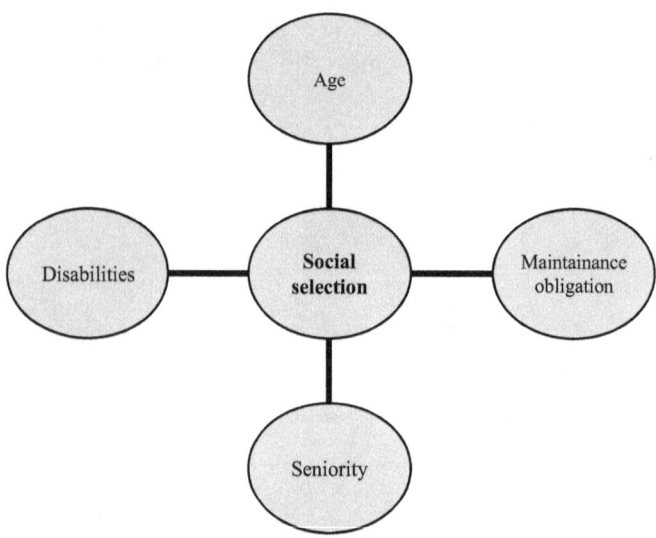

The decision must also be taken with a view to all comparable workers. The purpose of this selection is to identify the employee who will likely be the least to make a termination and which is thus less worthy of protection; In the case of a business-related termination, the dismissal of an employee is carried out after ranking their worthiness of protection.

The so-called "service provider clause" of § 1 (3), 2 sentence, of PADA makes it possible to withdraw from the social selection, individual employees whose continued employment is particularly due to their knowledge and achievements, or to ensure a balanced social structure with a legitimate operational interest existing within the company. This means for instance that, an employee who has certain training; considered indispensable for maintaining the company, can be removed from the social selection process, provided that no other person can perform these tasks. It is also possible to define an age structure within a company, for instance a company having very few young employees meanwhile a large number of these employees are close to the pension age. Here, it is possible to control the selection so that the current age structure for example 5% of employees are between 20 to 30 years, 10% between 31 to 45 years, 10% between 45 to 55 years and finally 75% employees of +55 years. This is to avoid that a company should face a demographic problem after Business - related termination.

Based on § 1a PADA within the Business-related termination, a termination can be openly acknowledged. Here, the employee is offered a severance payment while at the same time waiving to take legal actions for protection against dismissal.

Person-related dismissal

The reason for a person-related dismissal depends on the employee himself. This can be caused either by a drop in productivity or the loss of a qualification - for example, a professional motorist loses his driving license permanently.

The decrease in performance is a common reason for a termination habitually used by a number of managers as particular evidence. Often the decision to terminate is based on a latent dissatisfaction with the achievements of the employee over a long period. But these observations are not the most important argument because beyond that, an employee owes the employer a performance in "average kind and quality". An employee likewise does not require being an absolute high performer, though wished by everyone. In addition, the employee must be given the opportunity to improve his / her behavior. It includes talking about the drop in performance at the right time and specifically identifies how to improve on the performance. Being able to subsequently have reliable indications for a termination; discussions should be recorded and handed over to the employee to sign by himself the transfer and the correctness of the content. You should definitely keep maintain the idea if the bad / reduced capacities on concrete things like quantity/ hour, number etc.

Be aware that for all employment terminations, a dismissal due to defective performance requires the highest preparation from you from meaning; a "quick shot" is not possible here. You must be able to perceive, assess and report back on work performance over a very long period of time.

Also, you must assist the employee in improving his / her work performance. This can be done through training, a narrower leadership or simply via improved communication. If you cannot or do not want to invest this time, it is often more appropriate in this case to negotiate with the employee a termination of the employment contract (see also chapter on cancellation agreement)

In addition to the abovementioned point of bad performance, illness can also be a reason for a person-related termination.

For this purpose, 4 case groups are been distinguished:

1. Frequent short-term illnesses: Disease-related absences are only relevant for a dismissal if they exceed the 6 week-period of remuneration paid in the case of illness.
2. Permanent incapacity for work: If an employee suffers from a disease that renders him instantly and in the future impossible to perform his contractually payable work, and still is not expected to recover within 24 months; we talk of a permanent illness-related absenteeism.
3. Disease-related reduction in productivity: As defined under permanent incapacity for work but with the limitation that the performance of the job is partially provided.
4. Long-term illness: dismissal due to an incapacity for work must have existed for several months. Here, the individual case is considered very special.

There are strict requirements for dismissals from the above mentioned case groups. There are three requirements:

1.) A frequent or prolonged illness which does not improve in the future (negative forecast of the future);
(2) Which will continue to be an unacceptable economic burden in the future or which could pose a disruption to the company's work processes;
3.) The consideration of the employers and employees interests must be focus against a further economic burden on the employer.

In addition, the employer must undertake an operational integration management program (BEM) to prevent redundancies.

Occupational integration management aims to overcome the employee's incapacity for work, to prevent new illness and to maintain the workplace. The obligation for occupational integration management results from § 84 para. 2 SGB IX. According to this law, employees who have been uninterrupted or repeatedly incapable of working for 6 weeks within one year were offered the company's integration management program through which the employee's participation is voluntary, and if in case the employee refuses; the procedure is immediately concluded or otherwise, the employee accepts the procedure according to the occupational causes of the illness and discuss related prospection about possible solutions.

Conduct - related dismissal

The principal reason for the conduct–related dismissal is the behavior of the employee. Since dismissal is the ultimate goal, the employee must be given the opportunity to recognize and correct his misconduct before giving a notice for dismissal. That is, to have is a timely personal dialogue with him and the wish for an improvement should be made clear as already described in the upper chapter: warnings. If there is no improvement in the situation, a warning should be given.

These grounds include behaviors for example: late arrivals, non-compliance with work instructions, bullying (as a manner), violation of company guidelines, etc.

> If there exist a competent works council in the company, the latter must under specifications be heard beforehand, stating the reasons for the termination (§102 WC). Thus any dismissal without consultation of the works council is ineffective.

Extraordinary dismissal

The extraordinary dismissal, also known as immediate dismissal or dismissal for an important reason, represents the extreme case of the conduct–related dismissal and § 626 BGB outlines the legal basis for its application. An extraordinary dismissal is permissible whenever further cooperation is not reasonable until the ordinary termination of the employment contract and until the end of the notice period. The decision for when such unacceptability is justified in the event of an invalidity of the extraordinary termination is highly individual and should therefore be pronounced with the addendum "in a timely manner" so as to be able to terminate the employment contract properly. Some typical reasons for an extraordinary dismissal are theft, sexual harassment, fraud and similar serious offenses. The extraordinary termination may only be implemented within two weeks after the employer has made aware about the offense. As a rule, extraordinary termination is also possible for employees with special protection against termination.

> Upon the event of an extraordinary termination, the works council must be consulted and due to the two-week deadline, the consultation process must be speeded up in order not to miss any deadlines.

Dismissal on suspicious ground

A suspicious dismissal is an extraordinary dismissal which is based on the suspicion of a criminal offense or a serious breach of task. Also for the suspicious dismissal, the two-week deadline in accordance with § 626 para.2 BGB is taken into account. Like in the case with the extraordinary dismissal, the start of the period is the date on which the employer makes as soon possible aware about the presence of the notice of dismissal.

The employer must demonstrate that he has taken all reasonable efforts to clarify the facts before making the suspicious dismissal. This is not only a matter of investigating indices that speak of the employee's guilt, but also of examining allegedly alleviating indictments on an equal footing. In addition, the employee must be consulted and given the opportunity to present his / her own material or to dispute the incident.

In the case of a suspicious termination, formal documentation is indispensable to be able to provide evidence in the case of a legal dispute. It is therefore advisable to send the employee an official invitation and to inform him about the suspicious moments already in the invitation. The two-week period is interrupted during the employee's consultation and as a rule, the employee has one week to respond to the call for comments.

Altered condition of employment–related dismissal

Variation of contract dismissal is established when an employer terminates an existing employment contract and at the same time offers an employment contract under amended conditions. In practice for example, this form of termination is used
if the place of employment changes as a result of a shift of the area or the drop of the existing workplace and the employee is to take a different place within the company.

The employee has the same legal possibilities as in the case of the change notice, like in any other termination. He may also accept the working conditions under reservation and at the same time lodge a prosecution against the employer. If the employee rejects the new employment offered in the notice of variation, the change notice terminates the employment contract.

Probationary period dismissal

A dismissal within the probationary period (maximum of the first 6 months of the employment contract) is possible under simplified conditions. Here, a shorter period of notice is allowed by the legislature and other collective agreements until after a waiting period of 6 months. Furthermore, no reasons shall be given for dismissal within the probationary period, neither against the employee representatives. The idea however that during the probation period no protection exists is incorrect. For example; the protection afforded to expectant mothers in accordance with the Maternity Protection Act already exists as from the first day.

Special protection against dismissal

As already mentioned in the chapter on ordinary dismissal, there are some groups of persons with special protection. The following groups of persons are protected under special protection:

- Members of works constitutional bodies
- Severely disabled persons and their representatives
- Pregnant women and women in childbed
- Employees in parental leave
- Compulsory military or community service
- Military recruit
- Trainees

Members of works constitutional bodies
Already selected candidates for the election of the works council have a special protection from the date of the establishment of the electoral proposal, until the expiry of six months after the announcement of the election results. This means that these persons cannot be properly dismissed. The same shall also apply to the inviting parties to company or election meetings, in which case the right to terminate until the announcement of the election results or for three months. The regulations are taken from § 15 of the Protection Act. The dismissal is basically possible for an important reason (that is the extraordinary termination), but the approval of the works council must be available for this purpose or a corresponding approval amendment by the working court.

Members of the works council are under protection during their term of office and until after one year, even after voluntary rescission. This case applies same to substitute members; the protection for the duration of their representation and for the duration of one year after their last representation activity.

Severely disabled persons

In the case of the dismissal of severely handicapped persons with a severely handicap grade of at least 50%, their coordinate is been approved by the integration office in accordance with § 85 SGB IX prior to the dismissal. Once the consent has been given, termination may be declared within a period of one month. In the event of an extraordinary termination, this must be declared immediately after the Integration Office approval.

Persons in a position of trust for severely disabled people

Ordinary dismissal of persons in a position of trust is excluded during the term of office, as well as up to one year after the end of the term of office.

Pregnant women and women in childbed

According to §9 of the Maternity Protection Act, dismissal is prohibited during pregnancy and until the end of four months after childbirth. However, the employer must then be aware of the pregnancy or childbirth or at most, two weeks after the receipt of the termination.

Employees during parental leave

It is not permissible to terminate employees during parental or maternity leave.

Compulsory military service / military recruit

Even though this group of persons is now hardly represented in the companies, enjoys the special protection against dismissal. They cannot be properly dismissed from the date of the notification of the dismissal notice until the end of the service or defense.

Apprentice
During the probationary period, the vocational training period can be terminated at any time without notice. After that, the vocational training contract can only be exhausted. However, the term "extraordinary" is applied to a very strict degree. The more advanced the training ratio, the more severe the standards of its application.

Exemption

Following the dismissal discussion, the employer may have certain interests in the fact that the employee no longer appears in the company and in the name of the establishment until the end of the notice period. This can serve among other things, the maintenance of the company's peace (employees are dissatisfied and provide restlessness) and the economic interests of the employer (employees migrate to the competition). However, the employer can only refuse the employee's entitlement to employment if the interests of the employer are heavier than the employee's right to employment.

The exemption clause agreed with the employee in the employment contract entitles the employee to remuneration for the period of the exemption; for example, if the employee has a company car, he is allowed for a private use. An exemption often raises the question of whether the employee can be recruited by the employer during this period. Especially in the case of managers, the company car is often not necessary for the fulfillment of the function (function car) but is part of the salary package. Factually, the company car is not to be retained here; it can look different when it comes to authorized or service vehicles. These wagons are mostly necessary for the fulfillment of the task (which no longer has to be carried out) and have only been issued on the basis of this task. Here it is worth a deeper examination if the car can be reclaimed.

Employee directly link to exemptions and who regards the dismissal as unjustified will actively offer his labor force to the company as the opportunity to fulfill their obligations as stated under the contract until the time of the court proceedings.

If the reason for exemption is of economic interest, it is recommended to return the company's ownership such as the notebook and the Smartphone or to block the corresponding service accounts as the employee may also have access to sensitive company data during their exemption.

Notice of dismissal

The notice of termination is a unilateral declaration of intent and requires a written form. The terminating must ensure that the declaration of intent made in written form is received by the recipient. The access and the date of access are a matter of controversy in the event of termination.

So when is a termination considered? If the termination is handed over in person to the employee, the latter shall be deemed to have been received. It is recommended to have note of receipt from the employee by means of a receipt confirmation or an acknowledgement of receipt. However, it is not obligated to sign such a reception confession. Thus, in practice a letter of resignation is handed over with witnesses.

If a personal delivery is not possible, delivery is normally selected in letter form. The notice of termination shall be deemed to have been given when the recipient had the opportunity to take note of it though this is not actually legally relevant. The possibility of coming across the information exists at the moment when it was placed in the worker's sphere of power (insertion into the mailbox). The safest way is the delivery by a messenger, so that the messenger can be a witness to the access. The messenger should therefore know that he is giving notice of termination ("expert messenger").

> The delivery by registered mail carries certain risks. In the case of delivery via registered post, the recipient could not be present at the time of delivery and cannot collect the letter later from the post office. In the case of an enrollment, it is merely proved that "any" letter was sent.

Employee's possible legal actions

Since the dismissal is a unilateral declaration of consent, there is generally no consensus on the termination of the employment relationship or employment contract. In order to be able to take action against the dismissal, the employee must lodge a notice of protection with the competent labor court.

The complaint must have been collected by the Labor Court (§4 PADA) within three weeks after the receipt of a written notice of termination.

The Labor Court

The Labor Court tries through all instances to reach an amicable agreement between a plaintiff and a defendant. Only when this is not successful, the proceedings are terminated by a judgment.

Before the Labor Court, a check is made as to whether or not the termination is terminated or whether it is ineffective. If they are declared ineffective, the employment contract shall continue.

A dismissal is vulnerable to many points before court grounds, especially authorizing terminating employment contracts. Thus, often the right of the terminating party is questioned, the access or the date of the access is denied or it is stated that the termination is not to be recognized. In addition, deadlines are frequent points presented by the employer whereby possible shortcomings on periods of notice of dismissal or even for prescription periods are being examined and sanctioned by the work council. In addition, the social selection and the dismissal are the last options to take on court grounds.

The Labor Court procedure always starts with a conciliation hearing. The court sets an appointment and invites the two parties at the same time to adjudicate the action. The dates for the quality negotiations are timely and experience has shown that the negotiations are held within two to three weeks after receipt of the complaint.

The conciliation hearing is held publicly with no law enforcement. The trial is conducted by a judge of the Labor Court through which the judge discusses the dispute in factual and legal terms. He points out essential legal aspects and tries submits to the parties a proposal for an amicable settlement. If both parties accept this proposal, a settlement shall be concluded. The dispute is immediately cancelled after the conclusion of the settlement and at this point each party is responsible for their own costs.

If no agreement is reached within the negotiation, a chamber discussion shall take place. As a rule, the term for the chamber discussion is not as short-term as compared with the date for the conciliation hearing. The chamber discussion takes place before a chamber, consisting of a professional judge as chairman and two honorary judges. In the run-up to the Chamber proceedings, the two parties are to submit the relevant speeches in written forms within the period set by the court. In this case, the evidence lectures or speeches presented are also to be designated.

On the basis of the motions put forward and the previous written descriptions, evidences are been taken under during oral presentations which usually takes place during the Chamber proceedings and possibly require more sessions. Owing to the discussions in the Chamber proceedings, the Court will again try to reach an agreement between the parties. But If no conciliation is made despite an attempt to mediate, the court will settle the dispute by means of a judgment jointly taken by all three members of the board (chairman and two-seater). The judgment shall be promulgated and subsequently communicated to the parties in written from.

There is also no need for legal action during the first court proceedings before the Labor Court.

If a party does not agree with the judgment of the Labor Court, there is the possibility to lodge an appeal (§§64 et seq. ArbGG). The appeal must be lodged with the National Labor Court, which re-assesses the case from an actual and legal point of view. An appeal is always possible in the event of disputes concerning the existence of an employment relationship, concerning for instance the effectiveness of dismissals, the validity of time limits and similar. With the exception in these cases, a first-instance judgment can be made available for review if the Labor Court has accepted the appeal or if the complaint exceeds 600.00 €.

There is a need for representation in the case of appeals before the state labor court. Thus, the appeal must be lodged by a lawyer, trade union or employer representative. The deadline is one month from the date of the judgment delivery by the Labor Court. The justification for the appeal must be given within two months of the judgment receipt by the court of first instance. The composition of the Labor Court chamber of Appeals is the same as the Labor Court Chamber: a chairman of the profession as well as two honorary judges as assessors. There is also an amicable settlement of the dispute within the appeal procedure. If no agreement is reached here, the appeal proceedings are also terminated by a judgment.

A further complaint against the judgment of the national labor court before the Federal Labor Court is only possible if the Chamber permits revision. The non-approval of the revision can be return challenged within the framework of a non-admission complaint.

> Note that the court proceedings and also that of the labor courts are public.
>
> negotiations.

The Cancellation Agreement as an alternative to dismissal

The alternative to dismissal is often the conclusion of a cancellation agreement. In contrast to dismissal, this is a two-sided declaration of intent. Employers and employees agree to terminate the employment contract at certain conditions in the cancellation agreement. The employment protection legislation doesn't applies here and more also; the hearings of the works council is dispensed with. Often the cancellation agreement is the best option for both parties; on the employer's side, there is no process risk, and compensation. While on the employee's side, a future date for the termination of the employment contract can be negotiated.

The cancellation agreement is often offered instead of a dismissal if there are not sufficient jurisdictional reasons for dismissal is provided. Given that the employee is usually also aware of this, it is tactically astute to offer attractive termination terms.

A cancellation agreement may principally also be concluded after the dismissal is been pronounced. Important content points of a termination contract should be:

- The exact date of the employment contract termination.
- Settlement of outstanding payments (Christmas bonus, holiday allowance, variable compensation such as bonus etc.)
- Regulation on the remaining days of vacation
- Regulation on the job reference
- Clarify that the employment contract without the cancellation agreement conclusion would have been anyway terminated by the employer.
- Agreement on the amount and date of payment of the compensation
- Exemption
- Return of company ownership
- Silence agreement

- Other services such as career counseling, outplacement, further education
- Reimbursement agreement
- Exclusion of all other mutual claims

If the cancellation agreement was made after the pronunciation of the dismissal and an action had already been lodged with the labor court, an agreement on the withdrawal of the legal action should also be included.

> If benefits such as outplacement advice or further training are agreed within a termination contract, a tax liability may arise for this financial benefit. If the salary tax incurred is deducted from the employee, there is a regular need for discussion. It is therefore advisable to clearly in the cancellation contract the party who bears the taxation of the financial benefit.

The exit interview

Just as a company invests in the selection and recruitment of employees a lot of time, so it carefully should also deal with dismissals. Terminated employees can damage the reputation of the employer both internally and externally. Thus, it is important that the leadership in the termination procedure is a clear line and is fair to the employee. If the employee is treated fairly during the process, the employee will generally not seriously damage the reputation of the employer.

A notice of termination is a burden for all parties involved. Of course, there is the main burden on the employee to be dismissed, but also for you as a manager, this situation is challenging. Why is that? Initially, such a conversation is emotionally disturbing. But also they are under observation due to the external impact that it has on other areas inside and outside the company and which are not to be neglected. Your employees will also assess you in how you deal with such messages. A careful and intensive preparation of the conversation is an important factor for success. First, consider the following questions:

- What is the goal of the conversation?
- What are the justifying facts?
- What emotions play a role in this situation?
- What questions do I have to face and do I have answers to?

The more secure you can answer these questions, the more solidly you will be in the conversation. You will be more able to present your point of view and express yourself clearly and precisely. This is an important foundation for the conversation to be quiet and professional.

If you are in the situation of being forced to give notice of dismissal (personnel savings, etc.), avoid taking responsibility and blaming yourself on your superiors or "the head office". This neither helps the person concerned nor puts him in a better position. On the contrary, you only openly admit that you are not involved and just a command recipient. A more honest and professional approach is not only to discuss the concerns the decision entails for you, but also explain why you have made the decision to terminate despite these concerns.

If you are unsure and have little experience with it, do not be afraid to practice the conversation as part of a rolling game with a confidant. Many companies are preparing their managers for upcoming situations with upcoming training-related dismissals. Here the managers are equipped with arguments and the conversation is practiced with professional players. This has proven to be very effective in practice.

Of course, before you enter into an exit interview, all legal frameworks as well as the execution of the formalities (works council hearing, etc.) should be completed. The date for conducting the call should take place promptly. Because firstly, bad news is not better by waiting and secondly Increases each day and the more other employees; personnel department, works council, management and others know about the upcoming dismissal, the more likelihood the person concerned be informed over the office grapevine of his own termination. This would be highly unprofessional and not fair to the employee.

The conversation itself should be carried out face to face. Termination on phone, video conferencing or similar means is silent and not appreciative. Also, it should be a self-evident that you conduct the conversation as a leader. Do not delegate the call to the personnel department or to the next superior. Also the transfer of bad news is part of your tasks. Imagine these tasks as the only way to get the respect and credibility of your employees.

As a matter of course, the conversation should also take place in a confidential atmosphere. This means you need a quiet, not-for-easy-to-see, space. Mobile phone, telephone and e-mails are silenced during the call and will not be considered. The participants should ideally consist of you and the affected employee. You should be in an appropriate position if you want to get someone else in. This can be for example, the personnel officer responsible or your HR business partner. However note that, even if you have such support, the conversation remains in your hands as a sole responsibility. The added employee fulfills more the function of a witness or for moral support. In the ideal case, he expresses himself to concrete legal questions.

Make sure you do not bend behind your desk and the employee sits in front of the desk like a petitioner. It is best to choose a barrier-free seating arrangement, ideally on a round table or, if you only have an angular table, you will have a right-angled seating arrangement.

> A discreet, confidential atmosphere is indispensable for an exit interview. It creates the necessary professional framework protecting the privacy of the employee.

The conversation itself usually comprises four phases; these phases are usually of different lengths and do not necessarily occur sequentially. Often the transitions are blurred so that the phases are no longer to be separated clearly from one another.

1st phase
Termination and justification

2nd phase
Dealing with emotions

3rd phase
Looking forward and offering help

4th phase
Arrangements for further actions

Phase 1: Termination and justification

In Phase 1, the main focus is on leadership. This phase should start immediately after the usual greeting. Within the first five sentences after the greeting, the termination should be pronounced. They address the termination exactly and unequivocally and refer to the employee by name.

In order to give your message strength, it is important that you avoid as far as possible we-formulations. Use the I-wording to illustrate that you are behind the termination as a leader and thus identify yourself. This gives the spoken word binding and strength, as the employee perceives you as a leader. In a we-formulation, the employee can only perceive you as a messenger of the message and thus be tempted to win you as ally against the denunciation.

The welcome at the beginning of the conversation should be reduced to a minimum. The usual warm-up phrases such as "How's it going?", "how does the family do?", "Where do you go on holiday?", As used in normal employee discussions, do not belong to such a conversation and would rather be counterproductive because the conversation will take a strong turnaround shortly after these questions, resulting to a certain surprise effect and which is not appropriate for fairness reasons. The termination should be expressed in such a way that the message is absolutely clear. Nevertheless it should be transferred with fingertip feeling. The word "termination" or "dismissal" act severely. Use better phrases such as "separation", "dissolution of the employment relationship" and such like.

If you regret the step of the separation, you may express yourself in a timid manner, but please if you really mean it. Immediately afterwards you should name the reasons for the termination. Give the reasons clear, briefly and honestly. Avoid losing yourself in details. Provide that you can deepen the conversation on request at a further date. With all clarity and openness, please note that you are sitting in front of you a person who is receiving bad news regarding his livelihood. Do not put it in

the pillory, but formulate it gently and positively.
Avoid also placing yourself in a defensive position. At this point, the employee will have no compassion for you and your hard decision. So do as much as you can to stick with the employee's argument.

At the end of this phase, the employee must be clear that the termination is pronounced and can no longer be discussed.

Often the conversation is conducted in such a way that the reasons are explained first and then the termination is pronounced. The aim of this procedure is that the employee, after having heard the reasons, may himself be aware that a termination is justified. Unfortunately, this effect is very rare in practice. Rather, this approach creates a lot of pressure on both sides. Both know that something disagreeable will happen, and are tormented by the course of the conversation about whose end the denunciation inevitably stands. Through the direct utterance of the termination at the beginning of the conversation, the main event is equal and the tension is reduced.

> Leave no doubt that the employment relationship has come to an end.

Phase 2: Dealing with emotions

After or even during the speech of the termination, an emotional reaction is to be expected. There are four likely emotional reactions. The most important principle for you as a leader here is: stay calm and as a matter-of-fact do not become enmeshed. The four probable emotional reactions are:

1. Aggressiveness - attack
2. Dissociating - denial
3. Withdrawal - grief
4. Routine- rationalization

Aggressiveness - attack
Behavioral patterns here are typically;

O Insults
O Verbal abuses
O Stubbornness
O Threats
O Assault

If the employee falls into this reaction pattern, it is important to allow the feeling, but also to draw limits. At the very moment when the behavior tips in the area of a criminal offense, for example by threats or even an assault, you have to stop the employee with a clear signal in time.

Dissociating - denial
The employee appears to be working in this reaction. He reacts in a controlled way and does not allow the happening event approaches him. If he remains in this reaction throughout the conversation, it is important to make a clear statement of the

termination.

Withdrawal - grief
In this reaction, the employee usually relatively acts quietly. Often he is not able to speak. He shows sadness, fear and has the feeling of being surrendered. It can also happen that this employee cries.

This reaction is particularly burdensome for many managers. Leave the grief which also leaves the silence in the room too. If necessary, hand a handkerchief, provide a glass of water, and give the employee time to regain control of his feelings.

Routine – Rationalization
Employees with this response remain in the rule and begin to evaluate the negotiating position. They ask about the benefits paid by the employer, such as compensation and exemption. For this employee, a termination of the employment relationship is at this moment in order. He is now trying to get the best out of himself. Arrange a follow-up as soon as possible and clarify the termination conditions. If these conditions are conclusive and satisfactory for both parties, you can rule out the risk of a labor court process.

All these reactions are principally possible and often the terminated employee also experiences some of these emotions during the conversation. Try to respond to all feelings with understanding. Stay calm and argue objectively. You should avoid hurting or instructing the person concerned with phrases such as, "You cannot see that," "Stay reasonable." Do not stop the conversation when emotions are visible. Many counselors and seminars recommend concluding with the conversation at this point, but this may have a detrimental effect on the person concerned. Resist the urge to fill up any discussion breaks that may arise. Silence can help if the employee has to deal with an emotionally high-stress situation. So try therefore to remain silence even if it is difficult for you to bear the silence.

Dealing with the emotions is certainly one of the most difficult tasks for a manager in the termination process. You can only conditionally prepare for this moment. Everyone runs the risk of getting infected by the emotions in the situation because people are not robots and feelings must always touch us. This is why it is important to know in advance what reactions can occur. Try to find an "anchor" for yourself, so as not to get infected and remain in your role.

> A personal "anchor" is important in order not to be infected by the emotions. An anchor can be a picture, a song, or even an object to which you associate something positive. In the difficult situation, remember this picture, song or the subject and anchor yourself with it in order to be able to carry on the situation professionally.

Phase 3: Focus on the future

After the dismissal is pronounced and the motives for this have been put forward, the focus is laid on the future. The aim is to build up the employees concerned and to point out prospects. Try to activate the employee. Make it clear to him that he should concentrate on the future. This topic should only be addressed briefly in the notice of termination, since the absorption capacity for this topic will certainly be restricted at this time. However, this should be deepened in any case.

You may also be able to offer help, which may be part of an exit package; for example, coaching, outplacement, severance payments and exemptions. As a rule, this will not be the case for employees who are unsuccessful in their behavior.

If a larger number of employees are affected by a termination, a social plan is agreed with the works council. The advantage for the employee is that he does not personally have to negotiate individual components, but can use the services agreed for the collective body. In social plans, the following components are usually regulated:

- Severance payments
- Outplacement
- early retirement
- Transfer companies etc.

As already mentioned, one should only give a brief summary of the achievements in the exit interview. If the employee already has detailed questions, you can of course deal with them, but the majority of the separation package should be explained in detail in a further conversation.

Phase 4: Further action

The final phase is characterized by the administrative details of termination. In this case, further steps should be taken with regard to the termination and the existing withdrawal. As a rule, a follow-up meeting is also arranged. Important points within this phase are:

- handing over the notice letter and acknowledging the same by the employee or a witness
- Termination date
- Agreement on the internal communication to be carried out
- Any agreement on the exemption
- Deadline for a follow-up meeting
- Vacation and possibly overtime work

When handing over the notice letter, it is worthwhile summarizing the contents again briefly under the deadlines so that the employee can quickly internalize the contents of the writing.

> Employees are often in shock after notification of the termination. They only partially accept the termination notice. Gather the factual information from the conversation in a conversation log, so that the person concerned has the chance to recapitulate everything in peace.

> Bid the employee after the conversation to go home. Make an offer to give him a taxi on the company charges. Possibly, the employee is so agitated inside that there is an increased risk of accidents

The internal communication

After the exit interview, it is important to keep the information high. You can assume that relatively soon after the conversation someone in the company is informed of the termination. Thus it is important to start the internal communication quickly. For reasons of fairness and respect, you should give the person concerned the opportunity to inform the direct colleagues about the termination

It may also be that the person concerned does not want to take this opportunity and Perhaps because it is difficult for him to talk about the situation. Also, this maybe because he\she has to first deal personally with the situation at hand and hence, please discuss with him\her in advance what is the best approach for him. After the affected person has informed all the colleagues who are important to him, you should immediately inform the whole team about the employee as a manager. Do not go into details of the termination. Talk to the team about the future assignment of tasks and how to proceed. Through this open communication, you bend rumors. If the employee continues to work and is not exempted until the end of the notice period, make it clear that as a part of the team, he continues to fully enjoy all rights and obligations until latterly. This is to prevent exclusion from the team.

The official communication by the company and through you as a manager holds in the event that the employee legal disputes procedure against the termination carries a certain risk. If the employee goes to court and the termination is declared ineffective, you are faced with the problem of already informing the organization that the employee is to leave the company. A return to the company is therefore difficult for the person concerned, since he now carries a kind of "stamp" particularly if the term is a conditional termination which eventually makes further employment unpleasant for the person concerned.

An employee can cite this as an argument in order to win a higher sum of compensation. He then argues that the return is no longer reasonable for him. You being the manager in this case, it is a danger to stand as a "loser". So, weigh carefully what, how and when you communicate. If you are still in a hurry, take the employee out of the line of fire, release him, and argue that he is currently exempted from his / her actual tasks for other projects.

The withdrawal

The last working day is always the end of the termination. On this day, not only an employee, colleague and staff leaves the company, but as a rule also a higher store of knowledge. Particularly in the case of employees who had contacts with business partners, such as customers and suppliers, a "company's calling card" also leaves the company.

You should not let unplanned and unused the days until the last working day. A variety of interfaces such as the colleagues in the team of the terminated employee, colleagues from other departments, customers, suppliers and also the outgoing employees should be prepared for this day. In the previous chapter, we have thought about the internal communication. In addition, externals such as customers, suppliers and business partners, where necessary should also be informed. Existing knowledge about processes, projects and workdays must be passed on to remaining team members as well as documents must be handed over or returned. The transfer modes for material things such as company cars, computers, keys and others are standardized and regulated very professionally with exit check lists. The intangible things like knowledge and contacts are unfortunately often neglected. These are precisely the things with which an employee irrevocably disappears and cannot be procured as a tool during after-sales. Even though the termination was made on the bases of performance, there are many cases in the form of knowledge which the employee has. It is important for you as a leader to ensure that this knowledge is as comprehensive as possible to the company. Please also note that as a rule, the employee becomes more unmotivated when the departure day comes. This is only natural and often not a bad idea: the employee is aware that his last day is approaching and there is no longer an incentive for him to get involved. If there was disagreement between both parties for councellation and the relationship was permanently destroyed, this phase will presumably begin.

Therefore, make sure that you enter the transfer process as soon as possible. How do you design such a transfer process? Clarify for yourself with the following seven questions:

1.) What tasks has the employee performed so far?
2.) What did he perceive as responsibilities beside his main tasks?
3.) Who were his interfaces and contacts?
4.) What were there specific time requirements of the previous tasks?
5.) Which tasks are to be continued in the future?
6.) Who will take over this task temporarily or permanently?
7.) How and within which timescale can these tasks, knowledge and contacts be handed over?

At the end of these questions there is a kind of revised training plan with clearly defined responsibilities and times. Take the time and check the progress of this plan regularly. An extension of the handover period is not possible due to the employee's departure, so any delay is a potential risk to lose knowledge and know-how. Sometimes colleagues shows solidarity with the departing employee and delay the surrender process; "We will prove to the employer that it does not function thus". Be alert and clarify the situation as soon as it shows up.

The following show us more precisely the seven questions already pointed out.

1.) What tasks has the employee carried out so far?
Here is his core task. This is exactly the same as the job profile. However, this is usually no longer up-to-date and the task area has taciturnly changed.

2.) What did he perceive as responsibilities beside his main tasks?
This part is particularly interesting. In addition to their main tasks, many workers perform many small, unimaginative, but still important tasks. This is not untypical, for example a reception clerk is responsible for the complete support, administration and fitting of the meeting rooms, in addition to her core task which is written down in the job profile and specifically the reception of visitors as well as the mediation of telephone calls. If you concentrate only on the activities in the job description, you will be confronted with this reception secretary that there was more to carry out very shortly after the departure of the secretary. It is not uncommon to find that these "shadow tasks" represent a higher percentage of the workload than the main tasks. These tasks have simply been added over years, or have been carried out silently by the employer as these tasks are often neither process descriptions nor representation provisions. Here, the corresponding employee is usually the only knowledge carrier and also consider activities that have to be done only intermittently, for example once a year or once in the quarter. Often they fall under the table because they are not present.

3.) Who were his interfaces and contacts?
After the "what" has been clarified, the question arises, with whom the employee has interacted. Often, strong unofficial networks develop within the company, which can make the work considerably easier. This should be made visible now.

If the employee had contact with the outside, you should hold the presumed contacts for the transfer process and find further contacts by asking for further information. If your employee has had intensive customer relationship and is assuming that he is also working in the same job and branch office, he will not be happy to share his contacts. He will try to keep this knowledge exclusive and to make a profit with his new employer. Stay stubborn here to find out all the contacts.

4.) What were there specific time requirements of the previous tasks?

The focus here is to find out which quantity has to be transferred to other employees. This question is particularly important when only a small number of people are available to whom all tasks have to be distributed.

5.) Which tasks are to be continued in the future?

At first, this question seems somewhat strange if one were to believe that all the tasks be performed by the employee are of a specific importance and should be continued. However, it is worthwhile here to illuminate the task area to certain extend more precisely. Many tasks are carried out on the basis of a history, although the recipient of the work does not need the results for a long time, or the importance of some work has diminished. Use this opportunity to ask questions about the necessity and to remove obsolete tasks.

6.) Who will take this task temporarily or permanently?

After the quality, quantity and priority are been clarified, the question arises: Who can carry out these tasks? If a new hiring is required or if the remaining team can take over the tasks, it is important to take into account that the team currently does not have the qualifications necessary to perform the tasks. Thus it may become necessary to invest in appropriate qualifications. This should also be done relatively promptly in order not to overwhelm the employee who will assume the tasks right from the beginning.

In the event that the position is filled with a new employee, it may be necessary to delegate the tasks for a transitional period to the existing team. Check whether this is necessary depending on the qualification required for the vacant position, recruiting can considerably take longer than the employee's period of notice.

7.) How and within which timescale can these tasks, knowledge and contacts be handed over?

As the final step in the process, you should consider how the previously defined range of tasks can be handed over to the identified individuals. If there are already process descriptions in the company, it can be helpful to follow these descriptions when handing over and thus you should be realistic in the planning of the time requirement. Besides the delivery, the daily operations are still open for both the surrender and the transferee. Thus, both can spend limited time and energy on handing over and ensure that the affected employee receive the necessary open spaces.

The dismissal - an image killer wrongly performed

While the labor market was still an employer market a few years ago, an applicant was lucky enough to get one of the coveted job positions which have nowadays turned into many areas. Demographic change, globalization and mobilization as well as generation change, have caused the market more demanding for employers. Today, the potential employees must ask for specific information about their possible new employer, combed through the Internet, link-up with others and thus being able to gain a good market overview as employer's evaluation portals are becoming more and more popular. On these portals, current and former employees can assess their employer according to various criteria, especially employees who have not been professionally and fairly treated in the context of dismissal and left the company with a strong resentment. Through the evaluation possibilities, the former employee now has the chance to communicate the whole world their opinion about the former employer. With a lot of anger and feeling unjustly treated, this feedback wouldn't be particularly positive. If on the other hand, you treated your employee fairly throughout the process and communicated transparently, the lesser the probability of getting devastating feedbacks.

Beside the online feedback, there is of course the personal feedback, especially in smaller and specialized sectors. The probability of an employee looking for and finding a new job with a competitor after the termination of his\her employment relationship is relatively high. If he says that his colleagues are very negative about the previous employer, the chances of winning the company's competitors for their own company are reduced, particularly in the case of dismissals which are subject to the conditions of employment in which the employee is not responsible for the termination. It is therefore important to communicate transparently, to guide the process professionally and to accompany it and thus, places former employees as ambassadors of the company.

The reference letter

In the case of leaving the company, an employee is entitled to a work certificate. This claim derives from § 630 PADA. The certificate shall be issued on the day which the employment relationship ends. In this respect, one also speaks of a final certificate.

Employer references are important for the further professional career of the employee. The potential new employer is intended to facilitate the selection of employees and basically, a distinction is made between the simple reference one-side, which is merely a testimonial of the employment relationship and its duration while on the other-side, the qualified reference which also assesses performance and leadership.

You are obliged to submit the simple reference. A qualified employer reference must be issued upon the request of the employee. However In practice, a qualified employer reference is usually issued as much as workers do require.

If a simple reference has already been prepared in advance, this latter should be binding with regard to a final reference. If you wish to deviate from the assessment of the interim report, you must justify this by circumstances which have occurred in the meantime.

Keep in mind that references from an employer must satisfy the truth principle. That is, the content must be true and if the information provided does not correspond to the truth, you may be liable to pay compensation against the new employer.

On the contrary, the principle of benevolence must be fulfilled ensuring that the testimony must be formulated well because; it is intended to serve the worker's career. Due to the tension between these two principles, a specific language has developed. This language packs negative judgment into supposedly positive phrases. Nowadays, a well-known classic is the phrase: "Mr. X has always striven to meet our requirements." At first sight the sentence sounds positive. If you analyze it however deeper or knows the applied codes, one discovers that it meant that Mr. X has tried, but not with success. Or one expresses negative aspects by simply omitting certain things that are usually mentioned.

In a case where no agreement is reached with the employer and the content of an employer's reference is highly disputed, the employee may file a complaint for reference rectification. He must specify exactly which modifications and additions he would wish to have in the reference whereby the burden of proof is shifted on the employee.

Examples of the formulation:

Formulation	Evalauation
He has completed the delegated tasks to our fullest satisfaction.	Very good
He has completed the delegated tasks to our full satisfaction.	Good
He has completed the delegated tasks to our full satisfaction.	Satisfactory
He has completed the tasks assigned to him to our satisfaction.	Sufficient
He has by and large completed the delegated tasks to our satisfaction.	Inadiquate

Why is dismissal valid?

As you saw in the previous chapters, the termination process is complex. It contains many legal, social and emotional hurdles. In addition to these hurdles, the following idea also plays a part: Can I do this to this person? These thoughts and the above mentioned hurdles often ensure that no termination is pronounced. Many companies go for years along with employees whose work performances do not correspond to the ideas of the company or the management. This is both for the manager who gets annoyed repeatedly over the employee and criticizes the performance, and for the company that fully pays an employee but only receives a partial satisfaction from work performance, and also very unsatisfying for the team that has to iron out the uncompleted or wrongly work done of the colleague. Sometimes, the affected employee himself is dissatisfied with the situation.

A clear cut through a termination can be liberating for all parties. The company frees itself from an employee whose skills and performances level is no longer required in its form and can use the available budget for an employee with a more appropriate qualification. The manager proofs with the termination that he/she can solve the problems at hand though it is unpleasant and has the possibility to re-set the team. With this tough cutback, the affected employee finds the chance for a new start in another company. Oftentimes, I find new perspectives for those affected after a termination.

In many cases, the team is seen as a major obstacle as the manager is afraid that the entire team will be opposed to the decision and will show solidarity with the person concerned. This is relatively rare if the termination is based on the performance of the employee and usually, the team is glad that to be freed from the colleague. Such a decision often results in new dynamism.

All parties involved should also see a termination as an opportunity. The more you guide yourself to this idea, the better you can convince your team and the employees concerned of this idea. Hence conclusively, if you stand behind this idea, the decision to terminate in the future will be much easier to all the parties involved.

Volatile markets are changing demands on employees

In today's world of highly volatile markets, it is no longer possible to avoid dismissals as part of team development. The requirements in the companies are constantly changing. That is; if a certain qualification is very much in demand today, this can change within a very short time. If it is assumed that this qualification is not needed again in the foreseeable future, it makes no sense in the results-oriented leadership to keep it in the team. The place approved by the termination may then be filled with a person with a qualification currently required. However, perhaps it is also possible to take into account further training of the current job-holder. However, you should always ask whether the targeted costs and time are related to the profit.

Mixed teams brings the most benefit

Another important point is the issue of "operational blindness". Employees who work for a very long time in a company, perhaps even in the same position are in a state of disrepair after some time. The neutral and clear view of the work process often lags. In addition, employees who have long lingered in the company often give impulses from the outside. A new colleague brings knowledge about the processes and procedures from his previous company and will try to bring this into the new company and thus initiate an improvement. This does not imply that permanent employees have to be permanently exchanged for new ones.
A constant exchange would not prove itself but would rather lead to a lot of know-how from the company. Long-time employees remain important to the company; they know the company and the industry like their own western bags and not every idea that works elsewhere will work with the culture, the people and the

organization of the new company. The mixture between old and new employees, coupled with a future-oriented personnel development makes the recipe for success.

Cost of terminating an employment contract

A typical statement, which is always in the room, is: "You cannot dismiss it, it becomes too expensive." What is meant in this context "too expensive"? Examine the possible cost factors so as to make a comprehensive picture.

1.) Monthly salary
The monthly salary is still payable until the last working day. This also applies if the terminated employee who has been exempted from the work.

2. Social contributions
Employers' contributions to the social insurance scheme which are deducted from the monthly salary are payable.

3) Compensation
If compensation has been agreed with the employee or if the labor court has awarded the dismissed employee compensation, this must also be taken into account.

4.) Cost of recruiting
Costs for the recruitment process, such as; job vacancies, personnel consultants and internal administrative costs, must be set up.

5.) Cost of labor
As a rule, a new employee cannot be 100% applicable from the very first working day, he has to be trained, built up his network and "arrived".

Example of calculation
Employees given three-months' notice period by the end of the month, compensation calculation 0.7 monthly salaries per year of employment, seven years of service. New recruiting via HR consultants = 30% to a new annual salary of € 72,000 + 3% internal administrative costs, labor costs for six months with an average usability of 80%;

Type of cost	Amount
Monthly salary for notice period	21.000 €
Social contributions	4.200 €
Compensation	34.300 €
New recruitment	23.760 €
Costs of processing	7.200 €
Total	90.460 €

You can now easily apprehend know the cost of the termination, if you were able to award all the above points. In contrast, there are savings potentials that you can achieve with a new recruiting. These potential savings are defined particularly by the salary rate and the related social contributions included. Employees who raise the question of the costs of dismissal are more likely to have a long working relationship and a very high salary rate. Thus, most savings are to be expected here. A rather lower cost advantage will be achieved when it comes to the exchange of a very specialized expert. In this constellation, the supply on the market is presumably very low. This means that a relatively high salary will be required and that the recruitment may become more tedious and cost-intensive. Also, a long training period, in the case of an expertise which has to be trained at the workplace, could have a negative effect on the cost calculation.

In addition, a company expects more performance through a new appointment. At least if the termination is based on a deficit with the previous holder which could be due to an inferior performance in quality and quantity or lack of training. You must also include this multi-performance, which you expect from the new owner.

	Dismissed employee	new employee	Savings
Annual gross salary	84.000 €	72.000 €	12.000 €
Social security contributions	16.800 €	14.400 €	2.400 €
Performance enhancement 25%		-10.800 €	18.000 €
			32.400 €

In our example, the costs for the termination amount to a total of € 90,460. The expected savings amount to € 32,400 per year, which means that the return on investment is 2.79 yearly.

Conclusion

There are many important and delicate factors to consider when terminating an employment contract. The legislature has put some hurdles in the termination process which are envisioned to protect the employee from the arbitrariness of the employer and can also lead to a successful continuation of the employment relationship. The integrated escalation steps, such as a warning or the critical discussion described here compels the employer; represented by you as a manager on how to deal with the employee and towards the criticism played by him. If there were no legal hurdles, many work relationships would probably have ended without the two sides closely and consciously examining the issue accordingly. Also, even if the legal requirements appear complex, termination is not impossible. Knowledge about the process is the key to success in the event that the work relationship cannot be maintained, and being a manager; the key factor is for you to perceive the performance of the employee and provide timely feedbacks. The termination process begins well before the denunciation, usually with the ascertainment of misconducts and its corresponding escalation steps: feedback discussion, critical discussion and warning for a dismissal all require courage and a careful preparation. However, you shouldn't be afraid of it as a seemingly negative event; given that, the termination of an employment relationship also has positive sides which shouldn't be neglected.

Important legal extracts

The following are some extracts from the most important laws on dismissal issues. These extracts correspond to the status of January 2017. The most actual version is visible at the homepage www.gesetzt-im-internet.de which is hosted by the German government.

Protection Against Dismissal Act (PADA)

§ 1 Socially unjustified dismissals

(1) The termination of the employment relationship of an employee who has been employed in the same establishment or the same Company without interruption for more than six months is legally invalid if it is socially unjustified.

(2) A dismissal is socially unjust if it is not due to reasons related to the person, the conduct of the employee, or to compelling operational requirements which preclude the continued employment of the employee in the establishment. The termination is also socially unjustified if:
1.) In private law establishments
   a) the termination violates a guide-line pursuant to § 95 of the Works Constitution Act (PADA),
   b) the employee can continue to be employed in another position in the same office or in another office of the same administrative branch in the same locality or its commuting area, and the competent employee representative body has raised objections to the dismissal in a timely manner for one of these reasons, unless a superior representative body in negotiations with a superior office has not upheld these objections.3Sentence 2 applies accordingly if the continued employment of the employee is possible after a reasonable amount of re-training or additional training or under modified working conditions and the employee has given his consent. 4The employer has the burden of proving the facts which caused the dismissal.

(3)) Where an employee is dismissed due to compelling operational requirements within the meaning of para. (2), the dismissal is nevertheless held to be socially unjustified if, in selecting the employee, the employer has not, or has not sufficiently, considered the employee's seniority, age, tasks to Support dependents and severe disability;; at the employee's request, the employer must state to the employee the reasons on which the selection in question was made.

Employees shall not be included in the social selection pursuant to sent. 1 if their continued employment is in the justified operational interest of the employer, in particular due to knowledge, skills and performance or in order to ensure a balanced per-sonnel structure in the establishment. The employee has the burden of proving the facts which make the dismissal appear to be socially unjustified within the meaning of sent. 1.

(4 Where a collective bargaining agreement, a works agree-ment pursuant to § 95 of the Works Constitution Act or a corresponding guideline under the laws governing personnel representation stipulate how the social factors pursuant to para. (3) sent. 1 are to be evaluated in relationship to each other, such evaluation may only be reviewed for gross errors.

(5 1If, in the event of a termination on the basis of a change in business pursuant to § 111 of the Works Constitution Act, the employees who are to be dismissed are designated by name in a reconciliation of interests between the employer and the works council, then it shall be presumed that the dismissal is due to compelling operational requirements within the meaning of para. (2). 2The social selection of the employees may only be reviewed for gross errors. 3Sentences 1 and 2 shall not apply to the extent that the Situation has materially changed after the reconciliation of interests came about. 4The reconciliation of interests pursuant to sent. 1 shall replace the works council's comments pursuant to §17 para. (3) sent. 2.

§ 1a Claim for Severance Payment for Operational Grounds – related Dismissal

(1) 1 If the employee dismisses an employee due to compelling operational requirements pursuant to § l para. (2) sent. 1 and the employee does not petition the Labor Court to find that the employment relationship has not been dissolved due to the termination by the expiration of the period set forth in § 4 sent. 1, the employee shall have a claim to a severance payment upon expiration of the notice period for dismissal.

(2) The severance pay shall amount to 0.5 monthly remuneration for each year the employment relationship existed. 2§ 10 para. (3) Applies mutatis mutandis. 3 In calculating the duration of the employment relationship, a period of more than six months shall be rounded up to a full year.

§ 2 Modified Conditions of Employment – related Dismissal

Where the employer terminates the employment relationship and, in connection with the dismissal, offers the employee continued employment under modified working conditions, the employee may accept this offer subject to the proviso that the modified working conditions are not socially unjustified (§ 1 para. (2) sent. 1 to 3, para. (3) sent. 1 and 2). 2The employee must declare this proviso to the employer within the dismissal notice period, at the latest, however, within three weeks after having been given notice of dismissal.

§ 4 Seeking Redress in the Labor Court

Where an employee wishes to assert a claim that his dismissal is socially unjustified or legally invalid on other grounds, he must petition the Labor Court within three weeks after receiving the written termination notice to find that the employment relationship has not been dissolved due to the termination. 2If § 2 is the case, the petition shall seek a finding that the modified working conditions are socially unjustified or legally invalid on other grounds. 3Where an employee has submitted an objection to the works council (§ 3), he should include the position of the works council with the complaint. 4To the extent the dismissal requires the approval of an authority, the time period for seeking redress in the Labor Court shall commence only once the employee has been notified of the decision of such authority.

Work constitution Act

§ 95 Selection Guidelines

(1) Guidelines for the selection of employees for recruitment transfer, regarding and dismissal shall require the approval of the works council. If no agreement is reached on the guidelines or their contents, the employer may apply to the conciliation committee for a decision. The award of the conciliation committee shall take the place of an agreement between the employer and the works council.

(2) In establishments with more than 500 employees the works council may request the drawing up of guidelines on the technical, personal and social criteria to be applied in taking the measures referred to in the first sentence of the preceding subsection. If no agreement is reached on the guidelines or their contents, the matter shall be decided by the conciliation committee. The award of the conciliation committee shall take the place of an agreement between the employer and the works council.

(3) For the purposes of this Act a transfer means assignment to another work area which is expected to continue for more than one month or involves a substantial change in the conditions in which the work is to be performed. In the case of employees who are not, by the nature of their employment relationship, as a rule permanently employed on the same job, the assignment of the job to be performed shall not be deemed to constitute a transfer.

§ 102 Co-determination in the case of dismissal

(1) The works council shall be consulted before every dismissal. The employer shall indicate to the works council the reasons for dismissal. Any notice of dismissal that is given without consulting the works council shall be null and void.

(2)) If the works council has objections to a routine dismissal, it shall notify the employer in writing within a week giving its reasons. If it does not report its objections within the said time limit, it shall be deemed to have given its consent to the dismissal. If the works council has objections against an exceptional dismissal, it shall notify the employer in writing immediately and at any rate not later than within three days, giving its reasons. The works council shall consult the employee concerned before it takes a stand, in so far as this appears necessary. The third sentence of § 99 (1) shall apply, mutatis mutandis.

(3) The works council may oppose a routine dismissal within the time limit specified in the first sentence of subsection (2) in the following cases:

1. if the employer in selecting the employee to be dismissed disregarded or did not take sufficient account of social aspects;
2. if the dismissal amounted to non-observance of a guideline covered by section 95;
3. if the employee whose dismissal is being envisaged could be kept on at another job in the same establishment or in another establishment of the same company;
4. if the employee could be kept on after a reasonable amount of retraining or further training; or
5. if the employee could be kept on after a change in the terms of his contract and he has indicated his agreement to such change.

(4) If the employer gives notice of dismissal although the works council has lodged objections to such dismissal under subsection (3), he shall append a copy of the works council's point of view to the notice of dismissal sent to the employee.

(5) If the works council has lodged an objection to a routine dismissal within the period and in the manner prescribed and if the employee has brought an action under the Protection against Dismissal Act for a declaration that the employment relationship has not been dissolved by the notice of dismissal, the employer shall be bound to keep the employee in his employment at the latter's request after expiry of the term of notice until a final decision is given on the

case at issue; during such period he shall not make any change in his conditions

of work. On application by the employer the court may issue an interim order releasing him from his obligation under the first sentence of this subsection to maintain the employment relationship in the following cases:

1. if the action brought by the employee is not reasonably likely to succeed or appears abusive; or
2. if the continuation of the employment relationship imposes an unreasonable financial burden on the employer; or
3. if the objection raised by the works council is manifestly unfounded.

(6) The employer and the works council may make an agreement to the effect that any notice of dismissal requires the approval of the works council and that differences of opinion on whether a refusal of consent is justified are to be submitted to the decision of the conciliation committee.

(7) The foregoing shall be without prejudice to the regulations relating to the participation of the works council made under the Protection against Dismissal Act.

§ 103 Exceptional dismissal and transfer in special cases

(1)) The exceptional dismissal of a member of the works council, the youth and trainee delegation, the ship's committee and the fleet works council, the electoral board or of candidates for election shall require the consent of the works council.

(2) If the works council refuses its consent, the employer may apply to the labor court for a decision in lieu of consent if the exceptional dismissal is justified, all circumstances being taken into account. The employee concerned shall be a party to the proceedings in the labor court.

(3)) A transfer of the persons referred to in subsection (1), which would result in the loss of an office or of eligibility, shall require the approval of the works council; the foregoing shall not apply if the employee concerned agrees to the transfer. Subsection (2) shall apply, mutatis mutandis, subject to the proviso that the employer may apply to the labor court for a decision in lieu of consent if the transfer is warranted by important operational reasons, even with due

regard to the position of the employee concerned under the Works Constitution Act.

Civil Code

§ 622 Notice periods in the case of employment relationships

(1) The employment relationship of a wage-earner or a salary-earner (employee) may be terminated with a notice period of four weeks to the fifteenth or to the end of a calendar month.

(2)) For notice of termination by the employer, the notice period is as follows if the employment relationship in the business or the enterprise

1. has lasted for two years, one month to the end of a calendar month,
2. has lasted for five years, two months to the end of a calendar month,
3. has lasted for eight years, three months to the end of a calendar month,
4. has lasted for ten years, four months to the end of a calendar month,
5. has lasted for twelve years, five months to the end of a calendar month,
6. has lasted for fifteen years, six months to the end of a calendar month,
7. has lasted for twenty years, seven months to the end of a calendar month.

In calculating the duration of employment, time periods prior to completion of the twenty-fifth year of life of the employee are not taken into account.

(3) During an agreed probationary period, at most for the duration of six months, the employment relationship may be terminated with a notice period of two weeks.

(4) Provisions differing from subsections (1) to (3) may be agreed in collective agreements. Within the scope of applicability of such a collective agreement, the different collective agreement provisions between employers and employees who are not subject to collective agreements apply if the application of collective agreements has been agreed between them.

(5)) In an individual contract, shorter notice periods than those cited in subsection (1) may be agreed only

1. if an employee is employed to help out on a temporary basis; this does not apply if the employment relationship is extended beyond a period of three months;
2. if the employer as a rule employs not more than 20 employees with the exception of those employed for their own training and the notice period does not fall short of four weeks.

When the number of employees employed is determined, part-time employees with regular weekly working hours of not more than 20 hours are counted as 0.5 employees and those working not more than 30 hours are counted as 0.75 employees. The agreement in an individual contract of longer notice periods than those stated in subsections (1) to (3) is unaffected by this.

(6)) For notice of termination of employment by the employee, no longer notice period may be agreed than for notice of termination by the employer.

§ 623 Written form of termination

Termination of employment by notice of termination or separation agreement requires written form to be effective; electronic form is excluded.

§ 626 Termination without notice for a compelling reason

(1) The service relationship may be terminated by either party to the contract for a compelling reason without complying with a notice period if facts are present on the basis of which the party giving notice cannot reasonably be expected to continue the service relationship to the end of the notice period or to the agreed end of the service relationship, taking all circumstances of the individual case into account and weighing the interests of both parties to the contract.

(2) Notice of termination may only be given within two weeks. The notice period commences with the date on which the person entitled to give notice obtains knowledge of facts conclusive for the notice of termination. The party giving notice must notify the other party, on demand, of the reason for notice of termination without undue delay in writing.

§ 630 Duty to provide a reference

Upon the termination of a permanent service relationship, the person obliged may demand from the other party a written reference on the service relationship and its duration. The reference must extend, on demand, to the services performed and conduct in service. The reference may not be provided in electronic form. If the person obliged is an employee, § 109 of the Trade Code [Industrial code] applies.

The Author

Christian Müller, born in 1982, has been involved in human resource management for many years. He completed his training as a wholesale and export specialist, and further on educated himself in Human Resource Management on an avocational basis and he studies Business Administration at the Middlesex University. At the Wismar University, he was trained as a systemic business coach. He is a Management Drives Certified Partner for persons and group profiles. His professional career path has already taken him to various industries: wholesale, metal industry, market research and the chemical industry. He successfully assumed managerial responsibility in the previous years, with a professional focus within  HR in areas: compensation and benefits, HR organization (development and reorganization) and Change Management. Moreover, he conducts successful leadership training programs on various topics: "Leadership Role", "Employee Communication", "Team Leadership" etc and being a coach, he unfailingly supports young aspiring managers in taking their first steps and as well, accompanies managers of all hierarchical levels as a coach in the fields of team leadership and decision making.

www.ingramcontent.com/pod-product-compliance
Lightning Source LLC
Chambersburg PA
CBHW020930180526
45163CB00007B/2953